Predators in the Wild

Wolves

by Anne Welsbacher

Consultant:
Lori J. Schmidt
Wolf Curator
International Wolf Center

CAPSTONE
HIGH-INTEREST
BOOKS

an imprint of Capstone Press
Mankato, Minnesota

Capstone High-Interest Books are published by Capstone Press
151 Good Counsel Drive, P.O. Box 669, Mankato, Minnesota 56002
http://www.capstone-press.com

Library of Congress Cataloging-in-Publication Data
Welsbacher, Anne, 1955–
    Wolves/by Anne Welsbacher.
    p. cm.—(Predators in the wild)
    Includes bibliographical references (p. 31) and index.
    ISBN 0-7368-0788-8
    1. Wolves—Juvenile literature. [1. Wolves.] I. Title. II. Series.
QL737.C22 W45 2001
599.773—dc21   00-009989

Summary: Describes wolves, their habits, where they live, their hunting
methods, and how they exist in the world of people.

Editorial Credits
Blake Hoena, editor; Karen Risch, product planning editor; Timothy Halldin,
    cover designer and illustrator; Katy Kudela, photo researcher

Photo Credits
Lynn M. Stone, 11, 12
Richard Demler, 26
Richard Hamilton Smith, 10, 16
Rick Hobbs/rickhobbs.com, 6, 8, 15, 22, 24, 28
Root Resources/Anthony Mercieca, 14, 17 (bottom left); Alan G. Nelson,
    17 (top left), 17 (top right); Walt Anderson, 17 (bottom right)
Unicorn Stock Photos/R. E. Barber, 21
Visuals Unlimited/Elizabeth DeLaney, cover; Ken Lucas, 9; R. Lindholm, 18

1 2 3 4 5 6 06 05 04 03 02 01

Table of Contents

Common names: The most common wolves are the gray wolf and the red wolf. The timber wolf and arctic wolf are types of gray wolf.

Scientific names: *Canis lupus* (gray wolf)
Canis rupus (red wolf)

Average size: Wolves are 5 to 6 feet (1.5 to 1.8 meters) long from the tips of their tails to their noses. They stand 2 to 3 feet (.6 to .9 meters) tall from the ground to their shoulders.

Average weight: Wolves weigh between 50 and 150 pounds (23 and 68 kilograms).

Habitat: Wolves live in the arctic tundra, mountains, valleys, grasslands, forests, deserts, and swamps. They often dig dens to keep their pups safe from predators.

Prey: Wolves hunt deer, elk, moose, bison, antelope, musk oxen, goats, sheep, rabbits, beavers, and mice.

Abilities: Wolves howl to communicate with other wolves. They are able to hear high-pitched sounds that people cannot hear. Wolves also have an excellent sense of smell.

Social habits: Wolves live and hunt in packs. All pack members help take care of pups. Wolves often mate for life.

In This Chapter:

*   Wolves live in packs.

*   Wolves can run long distances without tiring.

*   Wolves have thick, two-layered coats.

Chapter 1

Wolves

Wolves are social animals. Most wolves live and hunt in packs. Packs often have five to eight members. But a pack can range in size from two to 25 wolves.

Wolf Species

Wolves are members of the Canidae family. This scientific group of animals includes foxes, coyotes, and jackals. Dogs also are members of the Canidae family.

There are two main species of wolves. The most common type of wolf is *Canis lupus* or gray wolf. The second main species of wolf is *Canis rupus* or red wolf.

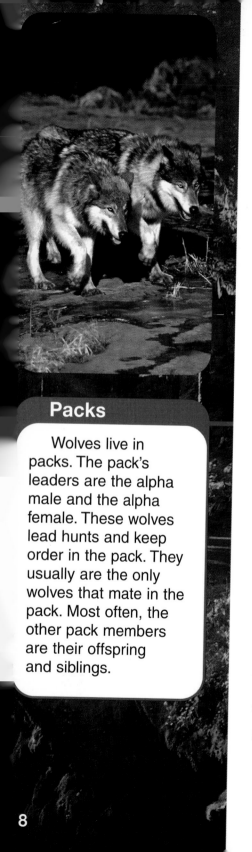

Packs

Wolves live in packs. The pack's leaders are the alpha male and the alpha female. These wolves lead hunts and keep order in the pack. They usually are the only wolves that mate in the pack. Most often, the other pack members are their offspring and siblings.

Appearance

Wolves have bushy tails, pointed ears, and long legs. They have narrow chests. Their heads are long and narrow. Wolves have powerful jaws to grip prey. They can crush bones with their jaws.

Wolves are about 5 to 6 feet (1.5 to 1.8 meters) long from the tips of their tails to their noses. Their tails are 13 to 20 inches (33 to 51 centimeters) long. Wolves stand about 2 to 3 feet (.6 to .9 meters) tall at the shoulders. They weigh between 50 and 150 pounds (23 and 68 kilograms).

Wolves often vary in size depending on where they live and their sex. Wolves that live in cold climates often are larger than wolves that live in warmer climates. Male wolves usually are larger than female wolves.

Red wolves have red coats.

Wolves' Coats

Wolves have many colors within their coats. Their fur can be white, cream, gray, red, brown, or black. The bottom part of their bodies is a lighter color than the top and sides.

A wolf's coat has two layers. The outer layer has long guard hairs. This layer can grow up to 5 inches (13 centimeters) long. It prevents a wolf's underfur from getting wet.

The underfur helps keep wolves warm in cold weather. This short layer of fur is thick and soft.

Wolves that live in cold climates often have longer, thicker coats. They have extra fur around their necks and on their backs. They also have smaller ears and wider muzzles.

Wolves have large paws.

Paws for Running

Wolves have large, padded paws with sharp
claws. Wolves' paws can be up to 5 inches
(13 centimeters) wide. The size of their paws

helps wolves keep their balance while walking on ice. It also helps them to walk on snow. Wolves' large paws work like snowshoes. Their paws spread their weight over the snow's surface. This action helps keep wolves from sinking into deep snow.

Wolves run on their toes. This running style allows them to stop and turn quickly. It also prevents wolves from wearing down their paw pads when running long distances.

Wolves spend much of their time running. They often must travel long distances to find prey. They may chase prey for 30 miles (48 kilometers) or more without resting.

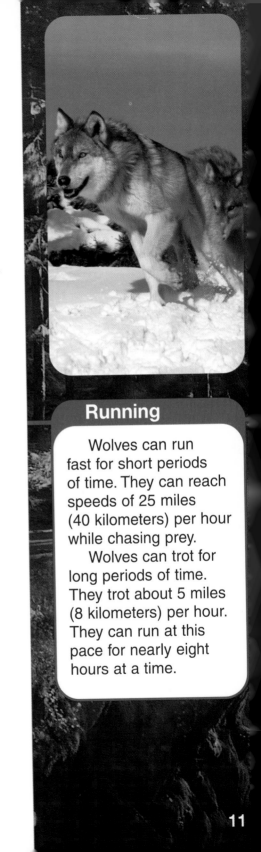

Running

Wolves can run fast for short periods of time. They can reach speeds of 25 miles (40 kilometers) per hour while chasing prey.

Wolves can trot for long periods of time. They trot about 5 miles (8 kilometers) per hour. They can run at this pace for nearly eight hours at a time.

In This Chapter:

* Wolves use their senses to hunt.

* Wolves often hunt at night.

* Wolves often hunt sick, weak, or old animals.

Chapter 2

The Hunt

Wolves are carnivores. They eat meat. In packs, wolves often hunt large prey. These animals may include deer, moose, antelope, caribou, and elk. Alone, wolves usually hunt smaller prey such as mice, rabbits, and beavers.

Wolves' Senses

Wolves hear well. They can hear another wolf howl more than 3 miles (5 kilometers) away. They can hear mice crawling underneath snow. Wolves also can hear high-pitched sounds that people cannot hear.

A lone wolf often hunts small prey.

Wolves have an excellent sense of smell. Their noses have about 200 million scent cells. People's noses only have about 5 million scent cells. Wolves can smell other animals more than 1 mile (1.6 kilometers) away. They also can smell buried objects and animals.

Wolves learn about prey from what they smell. They can tell what animals have passed through an area. They also know how many animals were in a group.

The Hunt

Wolves hunt at different times. During the winter, they hunt both day and night. During the summer, they often hunt after the sun sets. It is cooler then. Also, most of the animals that they hunt are active at night.

Most large prey animals travel in herds. A lone wolf can catch a rabbit or a mouse. But it cannot kill most herd animals. These animals are larger than wolves. Wolves work together in packs to hunt herd animals.

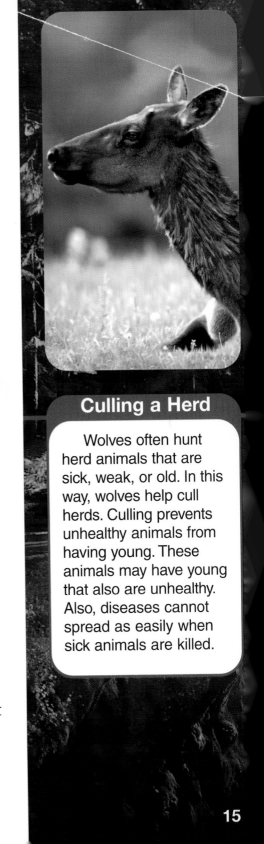

Culling a Herd

Wolves often hunt herd animals that are sick, weak, or old. In this way, wolves help cull herds. Culling prevents unhealthy animals from having young. These animals may have young that also are unhealthy. Also, diseases cannot spread as easily when sick animals are killed.

Wolves may chase prey for several hours or days.

The Chase

Wolves gather near the herd when they find prey. They watch for weak or hurt animals. When they find one, they surround this animal and try to separate it from the herd. They then chase it until it tires. A chase can take hours or even days.

Wolves take turns chasing prey. One wolf chases the prey. The rest of the pack runs at a slower pace behind the prey to save energy. Another wolf then takes the first wolf's place when it becomes tired.

Wolves may give up if the chase takes too long. Wolves catch their prey only once in every 10 tries. Wolves can go without eating for as long as two weeks.

What Wolves Eat

Deer

Rabbits

Mice

Elk

In This Chapter:

* Wolf packs surround large prey.

* Wolves can crush bones.

* Wolf packs share food with their pups.

Chapter 3

The Kill

Wolves circle around their prey. One wolf may lunge at the prey's nose or head. Other wolves then bite at its stomach, rear, neck, or throat. The pack attacks areas away from the animal's hooves to avoid being injured.

The pack's alpha male and female eat first. The rest of the pack eats after these wolves have had their fill. Each wolf guards its food by growling, baring its teeth, and making facial gestures.

Young wolf pups are not involved in the hunt. They stay in a den or in another safe area while the adult wolves hunt. After a successful hunt, the adults bring the pups food.

Teeth

Wolves' teeth are designed for eating meat. Canine teeth grab and hold prey. These pointed teeth can grow as long as 2.5 inches (6.3 centimeters). Carnassial teeth shear and slice the meat. These side teeth cut like scissors. Incisors strip the meat from the bones. Molars chew the meat. These flat teeth are in the back of wolves' mouths.

Wolves have strong jaw muscles. Wolves can crush bones with their teeth and jaws.

Eating

Wolves eat almost every part of an animal. They eat their prey's internal organs. These organs include the heart, liver, and intestines. Wolves also eat bone marrow. This soft substance in bones produces blood cells.

Wolves eat as much as they can during a feeding. A long period of time may pass between successful hunts. Wolves may eat as much as 20 percent of their body weight in one feeding.

Wolves sometimes cache large prey. They bury the animals that they do not finish eating.

Wolves' powerful jaws and teeth allow them to crush bones.

They then return and finish eating these animals later.

After they have eaten, wolves drink a great deal of water. The water helps them digest any hair and bones that they may have eaten. Wolves then rest. They may sleep for as long as 18 hours after a successful hunt.

Wolf Ranges

Each wolf pack has a territory or home range. This area can be 50 to more than 1,000 square miles (130 to 2,600 square kilometers).

Wolf packs protect their range from other wolves. Pack members mark their territory with their scent. They do this by urinating on trees and bushes. The scent warns other wolves to stay away.

Wolf Dangers

Wolves are at the top of the food chain. No animals hunt them for prey. But wolves still face many dangers. Wolf packs fight over hunting territory. Wolves sometimes are kicked or trampled by prey during a hunt.

Starvation is one of the greatest dangers for wolves. Nine times out of 10, they do not catch their prey. When they catch prey, wolves must guard it. Other predators may try to steal their prey.

Another danger for wolves is the loss of their habitat. People now use much of the land that wolves once used for hunting. This loss of habitat makes it more difficult for wolves to find prey.

Myth: Wolves hunt and kill people.

Fact: No healthy, wild wolf has ever killed a person in North America. Wolves often run away and hide from people.

Myth: Wolves are greedy and kill more than they eat.

Fact: Wolves eat almost every part of the animals that they kill.

Myth: Wolves howl at the moon.

Fact: Wolves howl to communicate. They may howl to warn other wolves of danger. They may howl to find their pack mates. Wolves also may howl before or after a hunt.

In This Chapter:

* Early settlers had negative views about wolves.

* People used to hunt wolves.

* Many programs now protect wolves.

C h a p t e r   4

In the World of People

Wolves live in many habitats. They find food and shelter in these natural areas. Wolves live in the arctic tundra. These northern areas are cold and treeless. Wolves live in mountains and valleys. They also live in forests, grasslands, deserts, and swamps. Wolves once lived almost everywhere on Earth. They had the largest hunting range of all land mammals except people.

Negative Views

When people started farming, they viewed wolves as a threat. Wolves sometimes killed farm animals. People then developed dog breeds especially to hunt wolves.

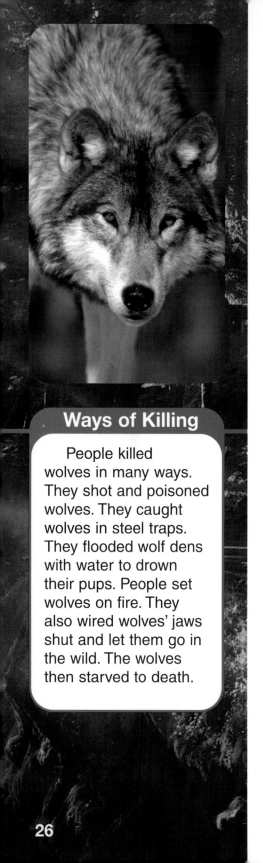

Ways of Killing

People killed wolves in many ways. They shot and poisoned wolves. They caught wolves in steel traps. They flooded wolf dens with water to drown their pups. People set wolves on fire. They also wired wolves' jaws shut and let them go in the wild. The wolves then starved to death.

In Europe, people told stories about wolves being evil. Many people believed wolves were witches or demons.

By the late 1800s, few wolves still lived in Europe. When Europeans came to North America, they brought their negative views of wolves with them.

In North America, people killed wolves as they settled new areas. Between 1850 and 1900, people killed more than 1 million wolves.

In 1907, the U.S. government formed the U.S. Bureau Biological Survey. This organization was created to find ways to decrease the wolf population.

Extinction

By the 1900s, some wolf species had become extinct.

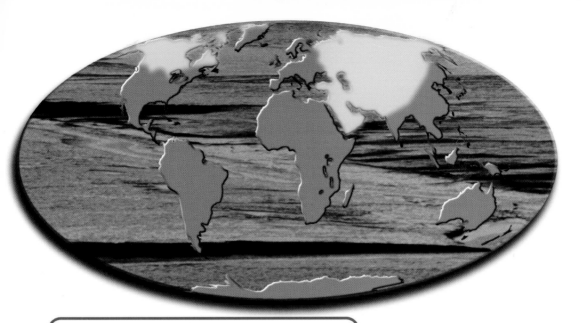

Yellow represents the gray wolf's range.

All the wolves of these species had died. Others wolf species were in danger of becoming extinct. Few wolves remained in Europe. Wolves no longer lived in Mexico or in much of the eastern United States and Canada. By the 1940s, wolves also no longer lived in many western states.

People continued to kill wolves throughout the 1900s. But in 1973, the U.S. government passed the Endangered Species Act. This law protects animals that are in danger of becoming extinct. Endangered animals cannot be hunted, killed, or hurt. Wolves were the first animal put on the endangered species list.

About 60,000 wolves now live in North America.

The Future of Wolves

Today, wolf populations have increased. Many states have programs to help wolves in the wild. These states include Idaho, Minnesota, Montana, and Michigan. In the United States, 9,000 to 12,000 gray wolves now live in the wild. Half of these wolves live in Alaska. More than 2,000 wolves live in Minnesota. Canada has more then 50,000 gray wolves.

In North America, people have many concerns about wolf populations. Farmers believe that too many wolves exist in the wild. They fear that wolves may kill farm animals. Some farmers want to be allowed to hunt wolves that kill farm animals. Environmentalists are concerned about allowing people to hunt wolves. They fear too many wolves will be killed. Wolves then may again be in danger of becoming extinct.

Some governments are developing programs to help wolves. In Russia, the government set up a large protected area for wolves to live in. In the United States, state governments are starting programs in Arizona, Idaho, New Mexico, and Wyoming. These programs protect wolves and help increase wolf populations in the wild.

cache (KASH)—to hide or store for later use; wolves sometimes cache large prey.

canine (KAY-nine)—a long, pointed tooth; wolves use their canines to hold onto prey.

carnassial (kar-NASS-ee-uhl)—a sharp side tooth used to shear and slice meat

carnivore (KAR-nuh-vor)—an animal that eats meat

cull (KULL)—to kill the weak, sick, and old animals in a herd

extinct (ek-STINGKT)—an animal that has died out; many wolf species are extinct.

habitat (HAB-uh-tat)—the place and natural condition where a plant or an animal lives

incisor (in-SY-zur)—a sharp front tooth used for tearing food

marrow (MA-roh)—the soft substance inside bones that is used to make blood cells

social (SOH-shuhl)—living in groups or packs; wolves are social animals.

To Learn More

Dahl, Michael. *The Wolf.* Wildlife of North America. Mankato, Minn.: Capstone Books, 1997.

Dudley, Karen. *Wolves.* The Untamed World. Austin, Texas: Raintree Steck-Vaughn, 1997.

George, Michael. *Wolves.* Nature Books. Chanhassen, Minn.: Child's World, 2000.

Horton, Casey. *Wolves.* Endangered. Tarrytown, N.Y.: Benchmark Books, 1996.

Useful Addresses

Canadian Centre for Wolf Research
P.O. Box 342
Shubenacadie, NS B0N 2H0
Canada

International Wolf Center
1396 Highway 169
Ely, MN 55731

Wildlife Science Center
5463 West Broadway Avenue
Forest Lake, MN 55025

Wolf Conservation Center
P.O. Box 654
Cross River, NY 10518

Internet Sites

Canadian Centre for Wolf Research
http://www.wolfca.com

International Wolf Center
http://www.wolf.org

Wildlife Science Center
http://www.wolftrec.org

Index